CONTENTS

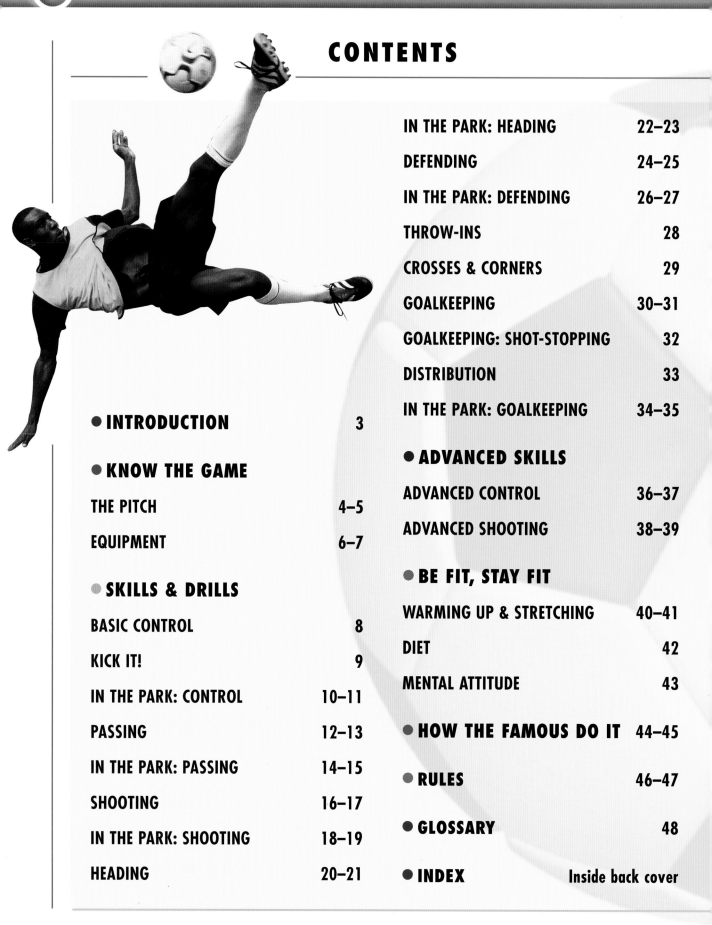

INTRODUCTION

I t is called soccer in America, fussball in Germany and voetball in Holland. In Spain it is known as futbol and in Italy they nip down the park for a game of calcio. Played in virtually every country in every continent of the world, football is the greatest and most popular game in the world.

GUIDE TO SYMBOLS & ARROWS

To help you understand movement and direction we have used the following ...

The red colour burst clearly demonstrates ball and body contact.

The orange colouring shows you the foot's point of contact with the ball.

The yellow arrow indicates the action of the body.

The red arrow indicates the direction of the ball.

The diagrams further clarify the action of the drill.

THE PITCH

Football is one of the most popular games on the planet. You can have a game in the park with four people, a ball and a couple of tin cans for a goal. Even a full-size game of football requires very little in the way of equipment.

THE PITCH

Not all football pitches are the same length and width. According to the rules of FIFA (Federation of International Football Associations), a pitch must be between a maximum length of 120 metres (130 yds) and a minimum of 90 metres (100 yds), and a maximum width of 90 metres (100 yds) and a minimum of 45 metres (50 yds). In other words, pitches come in a range of sizes.

CORNER FLAGS

Corner flags must be a minimum of 1.5 metres (5 ft) high for safety reasons and placed at each corner of the pitch.

GOALS

The crossbar on a full-size football goal is 7.32 metres (8 yds) long and the posts are 2.44 metres (8 ft) high. The post and crossbar must be white in colour so that they are easily seen. When sending the ball back into play, it must be kicked from inside the six-yard box.

TEAMS

A football match is made up of two teams of 11 players, each including 10 players and one goalkeeper. The teams can field their players in any formation they like. Substitutes may be used, the number depending on the rules of the individual competition. The home team usually has first choice of colours, and it is up to the referee to ensure that there is no clash of colours.

SEVEN-A-SIDE

Many young players will begin playing competitive football in seven-a-side matches on a smaller pitch, with smaller goals. This means they will get more touches on the ball and it is a great way to develop their skills in preparation for the eleven-a-side game.

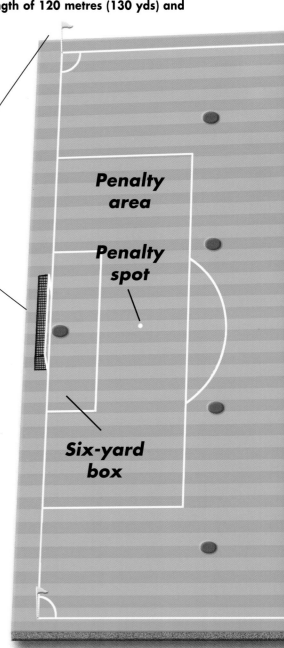

Penalty area

Penalty spot

Six-yard box

REFEREE

The referee is in charge of starting and finishing the match and enforcing the rules of the game (see pages 46–47).

ASSISTANT REFEREES

Previously known as linesmen, assistant referees are there to help the referee make decisions. They will use their flags to indicate throw-ins, corners, goal kicks and offsides, although the referee has the final say on all decisions.

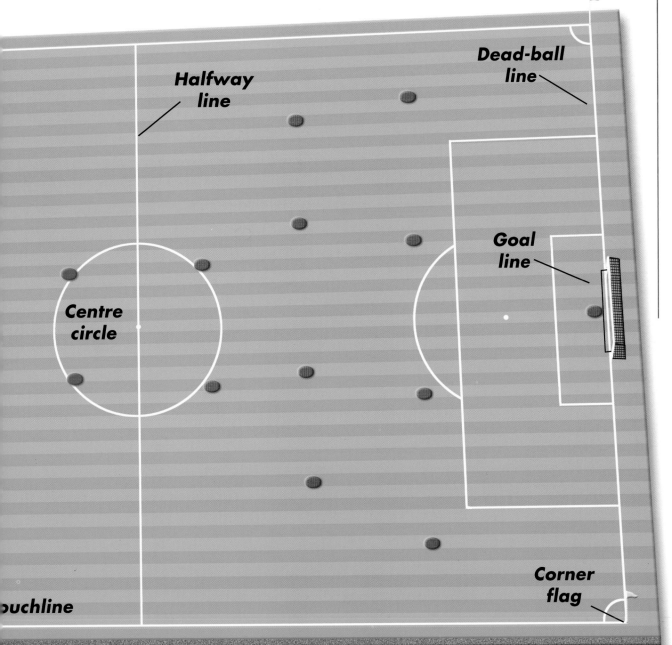

Halfway line

Dead-ball line

Goal line

Centre circle

Corner flag

Touchline

EQUIPMENT

*I*t is important to feel good when you are playing football, and that means having the right kit – that way, all you will have to concentrate on is the game!

SHIRT

Football shirts are made of light-weight material so they don't impair movement. Most also feature tiny air-holes to keep the body cool.

SOCKS

Football socks are big enough to stretch over a pair of shinpads and tough enough to give some protection to the foot, ankle and leg.

SHIN PADS

Players should always play in shin pads. Hard plastic on the outside with a soft cushioning material inside, they are often held in place by an ankle guard and calf strap, and then covered by a sock.

BOOTS

Boots are the most important piece of football kit and must feel right. Usually made of a combination of leather and plastic, they must be soft enough to be comfortable, but tough enough to offer protection to the foot. There are numerous designs, but always choose a pair of boots by what they feel like, not what they look like. Their sole should depend on the precise conditions they are to be used in.

STUDS: For use on soft and muddy grass pitches.

The studs (usually made of plastic with metal tips) come in varying lengths, pushing into the turf to give grip.

GOALKEEPING SHIRT

The goalkeeper's shirt needs to be stronger than an outfield player's as a keeper goes to ground far more often. They are usually long-sleeved to give protection to the arms, with built-in shoulder and elbow pads.

THE BALL

A full-size football is made from leather with a plastic coating to protect it. It has a circumference of 67.5–70 cm (27–28 inches) and must not weigh more than 450 g (16 oz) and not less then 410 g (14 oz) at the start of the match.

GLOVES

Goalkeeping gloves are lightweight but extremely strong. The palm of the hand area is made from sticky foam-rubber giving maximum grip. They are also designed to be substantially bigger than the hand that wears them, giving a wider surface area for catching the ball.

GOALKEEPING SHORTS

These are generally stronger than those of an outfield player and have padding around the hip area.

BLADES: A modern alternative to studs. *Blades are longer and thinner than studs. They are arranged in such a way as to give maximum grip and comfort.*

ASTROS: For use on very dry grass, astroturf and cinder pitches. *Astroturf boots have flat rubber soles designed to give grip on non-grass surfaces that don't take a stud.*

MOULDIES: For use on firm grass pitches and astroturf. *Moulded studs are made from rubber and are wider and shorter than normal studs. They give good grip on grass that isn't too soft or muddy, and can be used on astroturf.*

BASIC CONTROL

Keeping possession and preventing the opposition from taking control of the ball is the name of the game. That is why it is crucial for you to control it. If you have possession, it is much harder for your opponent to get it back from you and much easier for you to pass it to a team-mate or shoot for goal.

TRAPPING THE BALL ON THE GROUND

As the ball comes towards you, open up your kicking foot at a right-angle to the other one. As the ball meets the inside of your boot, bring your foot back slightly to 'cushion the ball'.

Raise your foot slightly off the ground to meet the middle of the ball.

ON THE CHEST

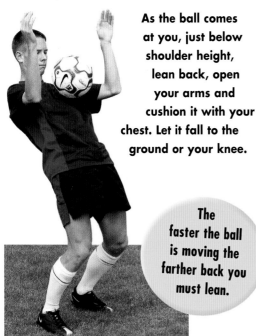

As the ball comes at you, just below shoulder height, lean back, open your arms and cushion it with your chest. Let it fall to the ground or your knee.

The faster the ball is moving the farther back you must lean.

IN THE AIR

When the ball bounces off the ground, get your body into position and raise your foot to meet it in the air. Cushion the ball and let it drop gently to your feet.

ON THE KNEE

As the ball approaches at stomach height, let it come into your body. As it nears the stomach raise your thigh to form a platform to cushion the ball, then let it drop to your feet.

KICK IT!

Now you've got the ball under control, use these four basic kicking skills to pass it on to a team-mate.

THE SIDEFOOT

Bring your leg across slightly and sidefoot the ball with a short, sharp action, punching the ball hard and fast along the ground.

STRAIGHT-ON VOLLEY

Approach the ball head-on using greater back-lift from your kicking leg. Kick it straight out in front of you, meeting the ball with the front of your foot, on the laces.

Always keep your eyes on the ball, your head still and your body as steady as possible.

THE DRIVE

The drive hits the ball long and into the air. Approach the ball from behind, swinging your leg back to get the power. Contact is made at the bottom of the ball to scoop it up into the air while keeping it low.

THE SIDEFOOT VOLLEY

To accurately pass a ball in the air to a team-mate, get into position as if to trap the ball in the air. Do not cushion the ball but play your foot towards it to make contact and re-direct it.

IN THE PARK: CONTROL

Here are three great drills to practise in the park to improve your ball control and balance. Try them either by yourself or with friends.

KEEPY UPPY (1 PLAYER OR MORE)

Playing keepy uppy in the park is a great way to improve your basic ball skills. Keep the ball off the ground, counting how many times you touch the ball before you lose control – then try to keep beating your record!

STEP 1
Try to play the ball with the front part of your foot, gently kicking the ball upwards.

STEP 3
You can play the ball with both feet, your knees, chest and even your head.

STEP 2
This will put backspin on the ball keeping it close to your foot. Also, try to use both feet, not just your strongest one.

TRAPPING CIRCLE (2–6 PLAYERS)

Stand in a circle, with each player a few metres apart. Then pass the ball to one another across the circle. Each player must control the ball with one touch, then pass it on.

CONTROL & VOLLEY (2 PLAYERS)

This drill will help you to control balls that come to you at an awkward height.

STEP 1

Two players stand a few metres apart. Player One then throws it gently to the other player, aiming anywhere between shoulder and knee height.

STEP 2

Player Two must control the ball, either with the foot, knee or chest, and volley it gently back.

TOP TIP
If you feel yourself losing control, spread your arms out to help you regain your balance.

PASSING

*F*ootball is a team game, so it is important that once you have control of the ball you can pass it on to your team-mates.

SIDEFOOT PASSING

Using the inside of the foot is the most accurate way of passing the ball to a team-mate. As it travels along the ground, it is easier to control when received.

STEP 1 *Step up to the ball with your non-kicking leg facing in the direction you want the ball to go and bring your kicking leg back.*

STEP 2 *Keep your eyes down and head over the ball as you bring your kicking leg forward to meet the centre of the ball with the side of your foot.*

STEP 3 *Keep your head and body steady as you follow through. The power of the kick determines the distance it travels.*

SIDEFOOT VOLLEYING

If the ball is off the ground, it is sometimes better to pass it on with a sidefoot volley than trying to control it and giving your opponents a chance to close in on you.

STEP 1
Steady yourself and meet the middle of the ball with the side of your foot.

STEP 2
Keeping your head down and your eyes on the ball, aim and follow through.

LONG PASSING

To pass the ball over longer distances, you will need to use more power and get the ball in the air. It is not as easy to be accurate, but a perfect long pass to a team-mate can give them an advantage over the opposition's defence.

STEP 1

Because you need more power, you will need to take a step or two back before playing the ball. Spread your arms to give you balance and step forward as you swing your kicking leg right back.

STEP 3

Keep your head down and follow through with your kicking leg.

STEP 2

Lean back very slightly as you strike the bottom of the ball with the front of your foot.

TOP TIP
It is always easier to play the ball in the direction you are facing so, where possible, turn to face the player before passing.

IN THE PARK: PASSING

E*ven if you have learnt the basic skills of passing, it is still important to keep practising. Pro players regularly use the drills featured here during training to sharpen their skills.*

PASSING SQUARE (5 PLAYERS)

A great drill for improving passing and ball control.

Four players stand in a square and one (Player X) in the centre. The ball is played to Player X, who traps it, turns 90 degrees to his right (or left) and passes it to the next player in the square. That player controls it and plays it back to the centre, where Player X controls it, turns 90 degrees and plays it to the next player. Swap around so that everyone has a go in the middle.

3-PLAYER PASSING DRILL

This drill enables you to play a long pass into the path of a team-mate on the run.

Three players line up in a straight line, 5 metres (16 ft) apart. Player B, in the centre, plays the ball to Player A. As he does so, Player C sprints forward. Player A must control the ball, look up and play a long pass into the path of Player C.

LONG PASSING DRILL (2 PLAYERS)

This simple exercise will improve the accuracy of your long passing.

Two players stand opposite each other, starting at about 10 metres (33 ft) apart then gradually moving farther apart. Play long passes to one another, lifting the ball in the air and aiming to place it at the feet.

PIGGY IN THE MIDDLE (4–10 PLAYERS)

Piggy In The Middle is brilliant for getting you used to passing under pressure.

All the players stand in a circle (the more players involved, the bigger the circle should be) except for one who stands in the middle (Player X). The players around the circle must pass the ball to each other while Player X tries to intercept. If Player X touches the ball, the player who passed it must swap places and go in the middle. Start off allowing each player one touch to control the ball before passing it, but then insist on one-touch passing.

TOP TIP
If you have more than eight players in the circle, place two players in the middle.

SHOOTING

You can't win a football match without scoring goals, so shooting for goal is crucial. Much of the art of goal scoring is instinct, reacting to a situation in an instant, but by perfecting your shooting technique you can increase your chances of success.

SIDEFOOT SHOOTING

Sidefoot shooting is for accuracy, when you've got the space to line up a shot and go for the corner.

STEP 3
Bring your head and upper body forward as you make good, firm contact with the middle of the ball.

STEP 1
Keep the ball position in mind as you line up to shoot.

STEP 2
Make contact with the inside of your foot, angling your body.

LONG-RANGE SHOOTING

To shoot from long range – anywhere outside the penalty area – you will need more power and height in your shot.

STEP 3
As always, keep your head down and your upper body forward as you follow through.

STEP 1
To gain more power you will have to run to the ball, turning into the shot for added strength.

STEP 2
Stretch out your foot as you kick, so that you make contact with the middle of the ball, on the laces of your boot.

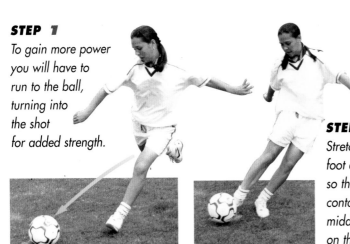

Volleying is a difficult skill to perfect. It is very difficult to time your kick so that you connect cleanly with a moving ball – but if and when you do it can be a lethal shot.

STEP 2

Anticipate the pace and direction of the ball, twisting your body as you bring your kicking leg round to meet it.

Keep your balance with your arms and non-kicking leg as you follow through.

Make contact with your boot laces and the middle of the ball.

STEP 1

As the ball comes towards you in the air, spread your arms for balance and get your body into a position early.

Chipping is another clever skill to use if the keeper is off the goal line.

STEP 2

Keep your head down and your body back. Approach the ball at an angle, plant your non-kicking foot virtually alongside it.

STEP 3

To give the ball lift you will have to make contact with the bottom centre of the ball, scooping it up into the air. On contact, stop the kicking motion; the stabbing effect should put backspin on the ball, lifting it into the air.

STEP 1

You do not need much of a run-up for a chip shot as you will require a delicate touch rather than power.

 TOP TIP

If you want the ball to go to your left in long-range shooting then, hit it slightly on the right and vice versa. If you hit the ball nearer the bottom it will go higher and travel further

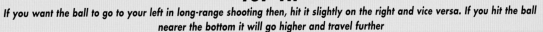

IN THE PARK: SHOOTING

*S*hooting is all about making the right decision on how and where to hit the ball. These drills are designed to help you get used to first-time shooting and hitting the ball on target every time.

TARGET PRACTISE (3–12 PLAYERS)

It is all very well getting the ball on target, but you've got a much better chance of scoring if you can hit the ball low and hard into the corner of the goal.

Place two cones or tin cans in a full-size goal guarded by a goalkeeper. The server, Player X, then stands on the edge of the penalty area. The other players stand outside the box and, one by one, pass the ball to the server. He plays it first time (with one touch) into the box for them to run on to and shoot, aiming for one of the gaps between the post and cone.

TOP TIP
Use the sidefoot shot in this exercise to give you the accuracy you need to hit a small gap.

LAY-OFF SHOOTING (3–12 PLAYERS)

This drill is great for developing shooting skills around the edge of the box, but it also trains players to react quickly to a pass from a team-mate before striking.

STEP 1

The server, Player X, stands on the edge of the penalty area. The other players line up back towards the halfway line. One by one they play the ball into the server and run forward.

STEP 2

The server lays the ball off into the player's path.

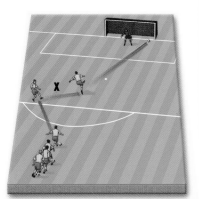

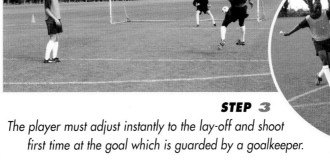

STEP 3

The player must adjust instantly to the lay-off and shoot first time at the goal which is guarded by a goalkeeper.

VARIATION

Rather than laying the ball off, the server holds the ball and bounces it into the player's path, meaning that he has to volley the ball towards the goal.

HEADING

Heading is an important skill to master, whether it be in defence or attack. You don't have to be tall to be a good header of the ball; the secret is timing and bravery.

BASIC HEADING

The basic principles of heading the ball are the same for attack and defence.

STEP 1

Watch the ball closely as it comes towards your head. Get your body into position so that you are right under the ball.

Aim to meet the ball on your forehead, keeping your eyes open and mouth shut, 'attack' the ball.

STEP 2

As the ball comes towards you, tilt your head back slightly and then nod it forward to meet it, tensing your neck, arms, back and leg muscles to make the contact strong.

JUMPING TO HEAD

Often to win a header you will have to meet the ball higher than head height, which means you must jump to meet it.

STEP 2

Time your jump so that you meet the ball at the highest point, attacking it with your forehead.

STEP 1

As the ball comes towards you and you judge that you will have to jump, crouch down to give yourself spring. If the ball is really high you may have to take a run-up.

BACKHEADING

Backheading is particularly useful in attacking situations, adding a dangerous dimension to corners and throw-ins.

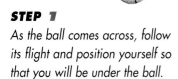

STEP 1

As the ball comes across, follow its flight and position yourself so that you will be under the ball.

STEP 2

Rise to meet the ball. Ideally you should try to meet the back of the ball with the top part of the back of your head.

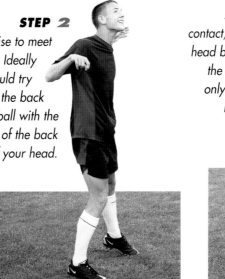

STEP 3

As you make contact, throw your head back so that the deflection is only slight – making it extremely hard to defend.

HEADING FOR GOAL

STEP 1

Get into position to meet the ball as early as possible so that you beat your marker to it and lean back in preparation to nod the ball goalwards.

When heading for goal, try and direct your header downwards as a low ball is much harder for a goalkeeper to save.

STEP 2

Get in a position (or jump) so that your head is above the ball. That way when you head it you can nod it downwards into the goal.

IN THE PARK: HEADING

These four simple heading drills are designed to improve and maintain your ability to deal with balls in the air. Just remember to focus on the ball at all times and be aggressive in dealing with it.

TWO-PLAYER DRILL

Two players stand 5 metres (13 ft) apart, one simply throwing the ball into the air for the other to head back. The players should repeat this 20 times and then swap roles.

> Don't worry too much about power in this drill, just try to make good, solid contact with the ball.

CLEARANCE-HEADING DRILL (3 PLAYERS)

In defensive situations you will need to concentrate on getting distance on a clearing header. Try this drill to practise.

Three players stand in a straight line, 5 metres (13 ft) apart. Player X (in the centre) throws the ball into the air to Player A. Player A jumps to meet the ball and heads it back over Player X's head into the arms of Player B. Player X then repeats the process, this time with Player B heading the ball to Player A.

 TOP TIP
When making a clearance header, getting power is more important than getting precise direction.

HEADING CIRCLE (PLAYERS 3–10)

Like all ball skills, heading can be used in many situations on the pitch. A good way of ensuring that you are comfortable in all heading situations is to play 'keepy uppy' in a heading circle.

Players simply stand in a circle 2–3 metres (7–10 ft) apart and must keep the ball off the ground, using only their heads.

Of course, in a match situation you can't expect your opponents to stand around and watch you heading the ball – they'll be trying to win it too!

HEADING UNDER PRESSURE (3 PLAYERS)

This drill is the same as the two-player drill, but with a third player who stands in front of the player who is heading the ball. This third player should not challenge for the ball, he should simply make things difficult for his opponent.

When heading under pressure take care not to foul your opponent. It is illegal to put your arms on his back or shoulders or push into him from behind.

DEFENDING

Defenders might not get the glory, but a last-ditch tackle or goal-line clearance can be just as important in winning a match as a spectacular goal.

BLOCK TACKLE

Pulling off a successful block tackle requires strength and balance as well as guts!

STEP 1
Get your body sideways on to your opponent and wait for the moment to pounce. When you can see that your opponent has lost control for a split-second or shown you too much of the ball, make a move.

STEP 2
Go into the tackle leaning forward over the ball so that your body weight supports your leg. Make contact with the ball with the side of your foot.

Focus on the ball. You must be sure you can win it if you're going to go for the tackle.

THE SLIDE TACKLE

The slide tackle is a tactic that requires split-second timing and great athleticism to pull off successfully.

STEP 1
Watch the movement of the ball closely as you run alongside your opponent. If you think you can clear the ball, launch yourself across your opponent towards the ball.

STEP 2
Extend your kicking leg and, as you slide across your opponent's path, hook the ball away.

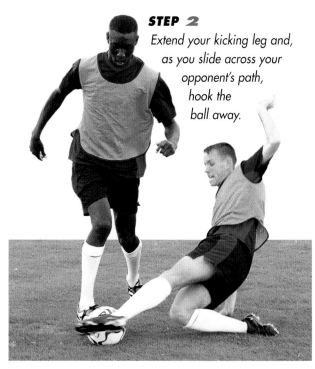

A sharp-witted defender will be able to run in and steal the ball from right under an opposing striker's nose.

STEP 1

Stick close to the shoulder of the attacker you are marking, but always keep on your toes, reading the play. If a chance to intercept the ball arrives, you are ready to pounce.

STEP 2

The ball is played in to the attacker's feet. If he is slow to move or the ball is under-hit you have time to step in front of him and steal it.

Do not attempt to intercept if you are not certain of winning the ball.

Sometimes as a defender it is too risky to try to win the ball. If your opponent has it under control, the best tactic can often be to jockey, to hold them up.

STEP 1

Position yourself in front of your opponent. You should block the route to goal with your body, forcing your opponent wide.

STEP 2

Continue to drop back, leaving the same gap between yourself and your opponent. Remain on your toes at all times, ready to switch sides or make a tackle if your opponent tries to get past you. Don't stand too close, or a clever opponent will be able to push the ball round you and get past.

IN THE PARK: DEFENDING

*T*he following drills are designed to re-create defensive situations so that defenders can practise their technique.

SLIDE CONE

In training it is not always sensible to practise tackling, because players can get injured if one is mistimed. This is a non-contact drill, however, and so carries less risk of injury.

STEPS *1, 2, 3*

The player must slide-tackle the ball without touching the cone.

JOCKEYING DRILL (2 PLAYERS)

This drill allows defenders to practise jockeying, encouraging them not to dive in and make ill-judged tackles.

Mark out an area roughly 20 metres (66 ft) long and 5 metres (13 ft) wide. Within this area mark out three gaps of 3 metres (10 ft) across as shown in the diagram below. An attacking player is given the ball at one end of the area, and must pass through the centre of all the marker cones to the end. The defensive player jockeys him all the way, staying 'goal-side', but he must not tackle at any point. It is the defender's aim to force the attacker to play outside the cones.

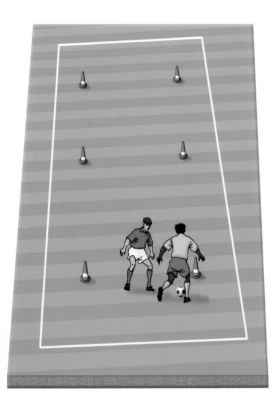

INTERCEPTION DRILL (3 PLAYERS)

By making drills like this competitive, you add an extra dimension to training.

Mark out an area of 7 x 7 metres (23 x 23 ft). An attacking player and a defensive player stand within this area, with the defensive player marking the attacker and the attacker trying to lose the marker. Another player stands on the edge of this box and must play the ball into the attacker's feet. The defensive player must try to intercept the ball. Whenever the attacking player collects the ball they win a point; whenever the defending player gets a touch before the opponent they win a point. The first to 10 wins.

THROW-INS

It is always important to keep possession for your team at a throw-in, which means the delivery must be right.

SHORT THROW

With all throws the ball must be held in both hands. It must go fully back behind the thrower's head and be released in one fluid movement above the head, while both feet are on the ground behind the touchline.

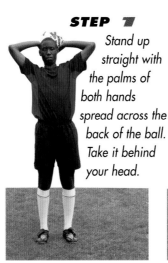

STEP 1
Stand up straight with the palms of both hands spread across the back of the ball. Take it behind your head.

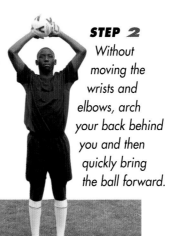

STEP 2
Without moving the wrists and elbows, arch your back behind you and then quickly bring the ball forward.

STEP 3
Release the ball when it is directly over your head and follow through.

LONG THROW

To get distance and power on a throw-in, you will need to take a run-up and put your back into it.

STEP 1
Having taken a couple of steps back from the line, grasp the ball firmly (with both palms across the back of it).

STEP 2
Begin to step forward. As you do, bring the ball back behind you and step up to the line.

STEP 3
Plant your leading leg firmly into the ground and, as you take the ball behind your head, arch your back.

STEP 4
In a steady and powerful motion, use your shoulders and arms to propel the ball back over your head.

CROSSES & CORNERS

People talk about great finishing, but often the greater skill is in providing the ball that has created the chance to score.

CROSSING

During a match it is quite rare to get into a good position to cross the ball, so when it happens make sure you put in a dangerous ball.

STEP 1 Approach the ball from an angle. If you are right-footed, approach it from the right and vice versa.

STEP 2 Spread your arms for balance and plant your non-kicking leg behind the ball.

STEP 3 Aim to make contact with the side of the ball. With this point of contact, and the angle of your run and follow through, your kick should curve the ball away from the keeper.

TAKING INSWINGING CORNERS

STEP 1 A right-footed player takes it from the left while a left-footed player takes it from the right.

STEP 2 He curves the ball in towards the goal.

By swinging the ball into the goal, you put the goalkeeper under immense pressure under his own crossbar.

TAKING OUTSWINGING CORNERS

STEP 1 Taking corners incorporates all the above crossing skills.

STEP 2 A left-footed player should take a left-hand corner and a right-footed player should take one from the right.

Swinging the ball away from the goal makes it risky for the goalkeeper to intercept, but perfect for an attacking player to score.

GOALKEEPING

*O*ne glorious save and the goalkeeper is the hero. Much of the goalkeeping art, however, is about good positioning and ball handling. If a keeper has these, often a spectacular save is not needed. There is no point being able to make incredible saves if you drop the ball every time you are called upon to make a simple stop or catch.

GATHERING THE BALL

Shots into the chest should be gathered into the stomach. If you stand up straight, the ball could easily bounce back out.

STEP 1

Allow your body to absorb the shot by bending over and gathering the ball in.

STEP 2

Once the ball has come into your stomach, gather your hands around it so it cannot escape.

BASIC CATCHING

When catching a ball at head height, it is vital to get your hands behind the ball, no matter how simple the catch may appear. It is these simple catches that can slip through a goalkeeper's hands due to a lack of concentration, so never think a catch is made until the ball is safely in your hands.

LOW STOP

There is nothing worse for a goalkeeper than letting a shot slip through his legs, so make sure it doesn't happen.

Go down on one knee, using your knee as a second line of defence should the ball slip through your hands. Your legs should form a 'K' shape. Then gather the ball into your body.

HIGH CATCHING

It is important to catch crosses and high balls into the box at the highest point possible.

STEP 1 Take a two or three step run-up to enable you to launch yourself into your jump.

STEP 2 As you launch yourself into the air, begin to extend your arms as you anticipate the movement of the ball.

STEP 3 Catch the ball and hold on tight. Be prepared for a bumpy landing, gathering the ball into your body as you fall.

PUNCHING

If the penalty area is crowded with players, you may not be able to get a clear enough run at the ball to catch it, so you may have to punch.

ONE-HANDED

One-handed punches are required when you need to reach over a crowd of players to clear a ball you can't catch. Clench your fist and extend your arm to its fullest point to literally punch the ball clear.

TWO-HANDED

The secret of a good punch is to make solid contact so you get as much distance as possible. Using two hands will give you a greater chance of making good contact. Clench your fists, hold them together and punch the ball at the highest point that you can reach it.

GOALKEEPING: SHOT-STOPPING

Good goalkeeping is about getting the simple things right, such as catches and saving. But a goalkeeper may need a little extra skill to pull off fingertip or diving saves.

DIVING SAVE

Shot-stopping is often a matter of instinct. It is particularly important to hold on to the ball after making a save or, if that's not possible, to push it out of play or away from the danger zone.

STEP 1 *As the shot comes in, shift your bodyweight to the side the ball is approaching. Position your hands early, ready to stop it.*

STEP 2 *Spread your hands so that your lower hand will stop the ball and your upper hand will come down on top of it to prevent it bouncing straight back.*

STEP 3 *Bring your body down behind the ball as an extra line of defence, gathering it into your chest as you drop down on top of it.*

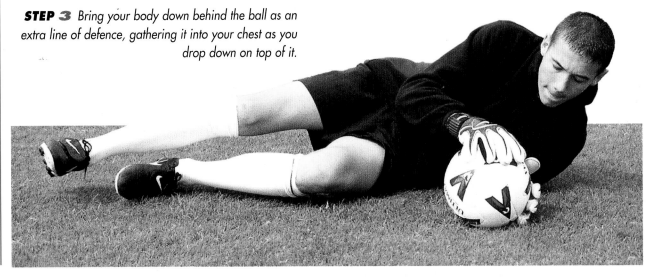

DISTRIBUTION

A goalkeeper who has good distribution skills can add a whole new dimension to his team, instantly turning defence into attack with a well-directed kick or throw.

HIGH THROW

Good for accurate longer balls.

STEP 1 *Lean back and twist your arm so that the ball is held above instead of below your wrist. Keep your arm straight as you bring your upper body forward and aim.*

STEP 2 *The farther you need to throw it, the earlier you should release the ball. Follow through to exert maximum power and direction.*

LOW THROW

For accurate short balls to a player's feet.

Swing your arm forward and go down on to one knee so that, as you release the ball, it rolls smoothly along the ground. This will make it easier for the player receiving the ball to control it.

PUNT

For less accurate but long-distance distribution.

STEP 1 *Hold the ball, cupped in both hands, ahead of you and concentrate on it. Take a two or three step run-up and release the ball swinging your kicking leg back as you do so.*

STEP 2
Focus on the ball as you kick it, aiming to get right under the ball to lift it into the air and across the pitch.

IN THE PARK: GOALKEEPING

Because goalkeepers sometimes have long spells during matches with little or nothing to do, it is important for them to maintain their handling skills and sharpen their reflexes in training. These four pro drills are designed to do just that.

BALL AT KEEPER (2 PLAYERS)

This drill is great to use in training to test a goalkeeper's handling, and can also be used before a game as a warm-up exercise.

A player stands on the six-yard line and, with the ball starting in his hands, drops it and half-volleys it at the goalkeeper. The keeper must catch it cleanly, gather it in and then return it each time. The server varies the height and pace of the ball with each delivery.

ON THE DECK (2 PLAYERS)

This drill is designed to work on a goalkeeper's handling skills, and also helps to build up agility and upper body strength.

STEP 1 The goalkeeper lies on his back with his shoulders forward and his hands set while a player throws the ball to him.

STEP 2 With the ball aimed to his left, right or directly at him, the goalkeeper stretches backwards or to one side to make the catch.

STEP 3 The goalkeeper rocks forward and returns the ball to the server in one movement, ready for the next throw.

CATCHING DRILL (3 PLAYERS)

It is all very well being able to catch the ball unchallenged, but it is a different matter altogether in a crowded penalty area. This drill is designed to re-create a match-type pressure situation for a goalkeeper.

One player, the server, stands at one corner of the six-yard box. Another, an attacker, stands in front of the goalkeeper at the far post, two yards off the goal line. The server must throw the ball into the air above the attacker for the goalkeeper to catch.

PUNCHING VARIATION

Goalkeepers should use the same drill to practise their punching, if possible placing one or two more players in the six-yard area to obstruct him.

 TOP TIP
If the cross is hit lower, to the front post or the centre of the goal, you must move towards the ball and get in front of attacking players to get to it before them.

ADVANCED CONTROL

Once you have mastered the basics of football, you can start to be more adventurous. Instead of looking for the easy pass, you can test your skills to the maximum.

DRIBBLING

Running with the ball under control, at speed and beating players can unlock the tightest of defences.

STEP 1 *The secret of good dribbling is to keep the ball close to your feet at all times. As you run with the ball, drop your shoulder and swerve your upper body. This will confuse the defender, or defenders, in front of you.*

STEP 2 *Move the ball from one foot to the other, keeping it as close to you as possible. If you can, use your body swerve and foot skills to wrong-foot an opponent and get past him.*

THE BACKHEEL

The backheel is not a difficult skill to master: the secret is being aware enough of the space and movement of your team-mates behind you to make it work.

STEP 1 *As you move with the ball and are aware that a team-mate is moving into the space behind you, simply move your kicking leg over the ball.*

STEP 2 *Kick backwards with your heel, making good firm contact with the middle of the ball.*

CRUYFF TURN

The Cruyff turn – named after the great Dutch player of the seventies, Johan Cruyff – is a good way of finding space when you are closely marked. The trick relies on the art of surprise to buy you some time.

STEP 1 Moving forward with the ball, stretch out your arms and lift your kicking foot as if you are about to kick the ball.

STEP 2 Instead, step over the ball with your kicking leg.

STEP 3 Twist your body back in the direction in which you came and at the same time flick the ball back with the inside of your foot.

STEP 4 Complete the 180 degree turn and move away with the ball.

THE STEP-OVER

The step-over is a great trick to use to get past a player.

STEP 1 As you meet a defender, move your kicking foot inside the ball as if you are going to flick it round him with the outside of your boot.

STEP 2 Instead of flicking the ball with your kicking foot, step over it. Hopefully this will confuse your opponent.

STEP 3 Shift your body weight the other way and flick the ball with your other foot to out manoeuvre a defender.

STEP 4 Run past the defender on the other side. Hopefully he will have been fooled by your trick.

ADVANCED SHOOTING

I t is very rare to get an easy shooting chance in football, and sometimes you have to do something quite special to score a goal.

OVERHEAD KICK

This is the one of the hardest football skills to execute, but when it comes off it can be truly spectacular.

STEP 1 *You can only attempt an overhead kick if the ball is coming across you in the air when you have your back to goal. If you think an overhead kick is needed, anticipate the flight of the ball, begin to lean back and shift your weight onto your kicking leg.*

WARNING:
The overhead kick is a move of extreme athleticism so be very careful when practising it. Make sure that you land on soft grass, sand or a mat.

STEP 2 *Focus on the flight of the ball as you stretch your arms out, continue to lean back and bring your non-kicking leg up.*

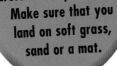

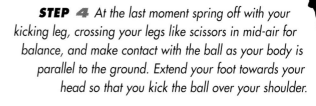

STEP 4 *At the last moment spring off with your kicking leg, crossing your legs like scissors in mid-air for balance, and make contact with the ball as your body is parallel to the ground. Extend your foot towards your head so that you kick the ball over your shoulder.*

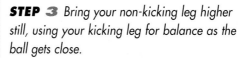

STEP 3 *Bring your non-kicking leg higher still, using your kicking leg for balance as the ball gets close.*

CURLING THE BALL

Curling the ball is another difficult skill. The secret is to strike through one side of the ball, putting spin on it as you follow through.

STEP 1 Approach the ball from an angle of virtually 90 degrees. If you are right-footed the goal should be to your left (and vice versa).

STEP 2 Shape up to the ball and strike it, aiming for the side, and make contact with the inside of your foot. This, combined with the twisting of your body towards the goal, will exert the spin that curls the ball.

OUTSIDE OF THE BOOT

STEP 1 Approach the ball from the opposite side to how you would if you were striking with the inside of your foot (right-footed players should have the goal to their right), but at a less severe angle. Strike the near side of the ball, with the outside of your boot.

STEP 2 Follow through in the same way as before, keeping your body forward and your head down.

TOP TIP

For curled shots that require height and distance, hit the ball on the side but towards the bottom; for shots that travel just off the ground strike the ball on the side, but more towards the top to keep it down.

WARMING UP & STRETCHING

*W*arming up and stretching before a training session or a match is very important. It lessens the chances of injury and increases a player's speed and ability to twist and turn.

WARMING UP

Before you kick a ball or even begin stretching, it is important to warm up your body. This dramatically lessens your chance of pulling a muscle or a tendon (the cause of more than half of all football injuries). All you need to do is a light jog for five minutes. This will increase your heart rate and get the blood pumping around your body.

STRETCHING

You must be very careful with your stretching.

- *Never stretch until the body is warmed up.*
- *Always stretch slowly and gently and never so much that it is uncomfortable.*
- *Hold each stretch for 10 to 20 seconds, keeping your body steady at all times.*
- *Never rock or bounce on a stretch.*
- *Breathe out as you stretch.*
- *Stretch both before and after exercise.*

There are many stretches, but here are some of the most important. Ask a coach or a physiotherapist to show you others, and check that you are doing them correctly.

HAMSTRING STRETCH

Kneel on the ground and stretch one leg out in front of you. Put your heel in the ground and your toe pointing in the air until you feel slight tension in the hamstring (this runs down the back of the thigh). Once the tension subsides pull your toes towards you for a further stretch.

PELICAN THIGH STRETCH

Stand on one leg, holding the foot of your other leg behind your buttocks with your knees close together. Maintain balance and stretch.

GROIN STRETCH

Sit on the ground with the soles of your feet together and your knees bent, pointing away from you. Then, using your elbows, press your knees down so that you feel a gentle stretch in the groin area.

TWO'S COMPANY

Some stretches can be done with a team-mate. This develops better balance. Keep the stretch steady and safe.

CALF STRETCH

Put the weight of your body on the front foot, bending the knee and stretching the other leg behind with the weight resting on your toes. Then lean forward so that your hands touch the ground, and slowly push your outstretched leg back.

DIET

You can't make yourself more skilful by consuming certain foods, but you can give yourself more energy and stamina on the pitch by eating and drinking a balanced diet. This food chart gives you the basic principles of a balanced diet, ideal for all athletes.

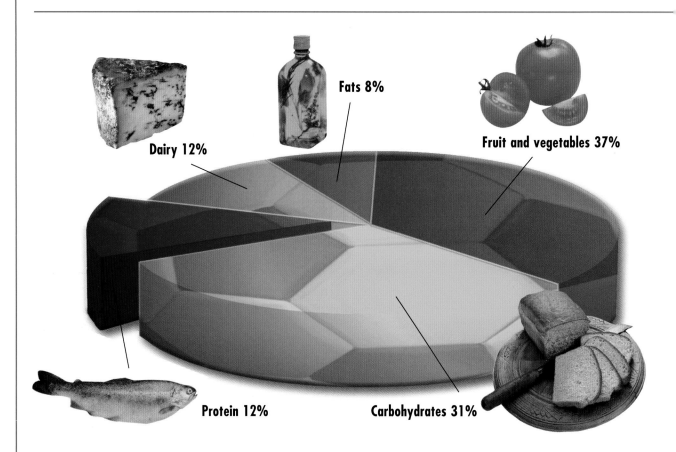

Dairy 12%

Fats 8%

Fruit and vegetables 37%

Protein 12%

Carbohydrates 31%

ENERGY BUSTERS

If you are doing a lot of exercise, then you need to cut down on fatty foods and eat plenty of carbohydrates to provide the energy for the exercise you are doing.

Protein is required for the growth and repair of the body, but try to choose low-fat sources.

BEFORE THE MATCH

To produce the maximum energy before a match or training, you should eat a high-carbohydrate meal at least three hours before the game.

Low-fat pasta or rice dishes (with no creamy sauce) are ideal. In the run-up to the game, boost your carbohydrate levels with fast-digesting snacks, such as bananas or dried fruit. It is crucial to drink plenty of liquid before a game. Water or isotonic sports drinks consumed two or three hours before playing will make up for the water you lose (through sweat) when playing.

MENTAL ATTITUDE

*A*s well as preparing the body, it is also important to prepare the mind for a football match and even training. Much of the skill of being a good footballer is to do it with confidence and self-belief. If you believe that you will score the penalty then the chances are you will.

MIND & BODY

The strength of a footballer comes from both mind and body.
It is important to do other forms of exercise to strengthen all areas of the body. Full physical fitness makes the mind more alert and decisive. Do not underestimate the level of concentration and quick-thinking that is required on the field.

MENTAL PREPARATION

Before a game you should focus your mind on the task ahead, visualizing certain match situations and how you would deal with them in your head.
Picture yourself scoring the goal, making the spectacular save or the last-ditch tackle. Focus your mind on the game as an individual player and as a team (it is the responsibility of the captain or coach to do this). If you believe you are going to win, you probably will. You will certainly have a better chance.

HOW THE FAMOUS DO IT

Imagine it, playing football every day AND getting paid for it! But don't think it is all glamour and glory; it takes hard work and dedication to make it to the top and stay there. The modern footballer has to maintain high levels of performance by sticking to a strict diet, cutting out alcohol and getting plenty of sleep.

TYPICAL TRAINING DAY

7.30	Wake up
8.00	Eat low-fat, high-carbohydrate breakfast
9.15	Arrive at training ground
9.30	Change into training kit
10.00	Warm-up and stretching
10.30	Training
	– Fitness work: sprints, circuits and jogging
	– Ballwork: Control and passing drills
	– Specific coaching: defence, midfield and attack
	– 11-a-side practice match
	– Shooting and set-piece practice
1.30	Shower and change
2.00	Lunch
3.00	Team meeting: discuss tactics for the next match
4.00	Home

TYPICAL MATCH DAY

9.00	Wake up
9.30	Light breakfast of cereal and fruit
11.00	Leave for ground
12.00	Pre-match meal – chicken and pasta
1.00	Team meeting
2.00	Get changed
2.15	Warm-up
2.45	Team talk
2.55	Leave dressing room for pitch
3.00	Kick off
3.45	Half-time
4.00	Second half
4.45	Final whistle
5.00	Post-match interviews
5.30	Cool down, then soft drinks in the Players' Lounge
6.30	Return home

TRAVELLING TO MATCHES

Of course not all matches are home games, and modern football players spend a huge amount of time travelling to away and international matches.

If the away match is more than 160 km (100 miles), teams will usually travel the day before the game and stay in a hotel near their opponents' ground. Then on the day of the match they can rest and focus on the match ahead, rather than sit in traffic on the motorway. For European matches, teams will fly out a day or two before the match. Players picked to play for their country may have to fly to the other side of the world for a game!

MONEY

Footballers in Britain's Premiership, Italy's Series A or Spain's La Liga earn huge amounts of money, but the vast majority of professional footballers do not.

The few that are at the top benefit from vast sponsorship deals and other spin-offs, but all of them would argue that their main motivation is the love of the game.

MEDIA WORK

If you are a top footballer, everyone wants to know your opinion.

There are hundreds of TV and radio shows, newspapers, magazines and websites dedicated to football, and part of the footballers' job is to do interviews and pose for photos. Some players enjoy this, while others hate it, but even in the lower divisions no player can avoid the TV lights, the radio microphone or the reporter's dictaphone for long.

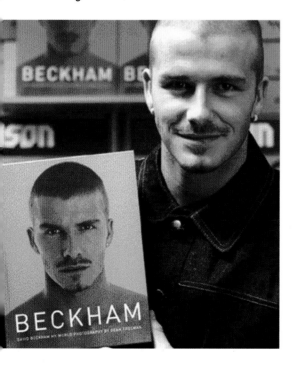

RULES

As with all games, rules are designed to ensure play is fair and safe. These are the basics, and they are always enforced by the referee.

THE OBJECTIVE

To score more goals than the other team. The winning team is the one that scores the most goals. If both sides score none, or the same number, the result is a draw. Whether a game goes to extra time, golden goal or penalty shoot-outs depends on the individual rules of the competition in which the game is being played.

TIME

A standard eleven-a-side football match lasts 90 minutes in two halves of 45 minutes, plus injury time at the end of each half (decided upon by the referee).

FOOT-BALL

The ball can be played by any part of the body other than the arm and hand. However, dangerous kicking (going for the ball when it is in the air and near another player's head) is not allowed. If a player is guilty of handling the ball or dangerous kicking, a free kick will be awarded to the opposition.

A GOAL

A goal is scored when the ball goes between the posts and under the crossbar of the goal structure, completely crossing the goal line (either along the ground or in the air). When a goal is scored, play is re-started with a kick-off by the team that has just conceded the goal.

FREE KICKS

A free kick is awarded by the referee when a foul is committed or a player is offside. A kick is awarded to the team on which the offence was committed, and all opposition players must be at least 9 metres (10 yds) from the ball when it is taken.

Most free kicks are direct and can be scored from, but certain offences, such as obstruction, merit an indirect kick. This means that the attacking team cannot score directly from it, the ball must touch at least one other player (on either team) before a legal goal can be scored.

PENALTIES

A penalty kick is awarded when a player from the defending team commits a foul against an attacking player inside the penalty area. The attacking team must nominate one player to take the kick from the penalty spot, while the rest of the players on the pitch stand outside the penalty area and the 'D'. If he scores, then a goal is awarded.

The goalkeeper may move along his line before the kick, but he cannot move forward until after the kick is taken. If he does so, the kick must be taken again. The penalty taker is not allowed to touch the ball again until another player (from either side) has done so.

OFFSIDE

At the exact moment the ball is played forward by an attacking player, there must be at least two defending players (including the goalkeeper) between or level with the farthest forward attacking player and the goal. This rule does not apply if the farthest forward attacking player is within his own half.

BACKPASS LAW

A goalkeeper is not allowed to touch the ball with his hands if it is intentionally passed to him by a team-mate. If he does so, an indirect free kick is awarded.

SIX-SECOND LAW

After a goalkeeper has picked up the ball, he must release it within six seconds. However, during that time he can take as many steps as he wants.

YELLOW CARD

Known as a caution, this is issued to a player who has committed a particularly bad foul or who has repeatedly offended. There are also certain offences that merit an automatic yellow card, such as deliberate handball and kicking the ball away after the whistle has blown.

RED CARD

If a player is issued with a red card by the referee he must leave the field of play immediately. Certain offences merit an automatic red card, such as fighting intentionally or handling the ball on the goal line to prevent a goal. If a player is awarded two yellow cards within the same match, he is automatically issued a red card.

GOAL LINE

If the ball completely crosses this line legally then it is a goal.

DEAD-BALL LINE

If the ball completely crosses this line, a goal kick or a corner is awarded, depending on whether the last player to touch it was an attacking player (goal kick) or a defending one (corner).

TOUCHLINE

If the ball completely crosses this line, possession of the ball is given to the opposing team for a throw-in.

PENALTY AREA

This is the only area on the pitch where the goalkeeper is allowed to touch the ball with his hands. When a defending player commits a foul inside the area, a penalty kick is awarded to the opposition (unless the offence is an indirect free-kick offence, such as obstruction or the goalkeeper handles a backpass. In this case an indirect free kick is awarded).

THE 'D'

When a penalty is awarded, all players (apart from the goalkeeper and the kicker) must be outside the penalty area, and outside this small 'D'.

SIX-YARD BOX

Goal kicks can be taken from anywhere within the six-yard box.

PENALTY SPOT

From where penalty kicks are taken. On a full-size pitch it should be 11 metres (12 yds) from the centre of the goal.

HALFWAY LINE

This marks the halfway point in the length of the pitch.

CENTRE CIRCLE

A circle with a 9 metres (10 yds) radius in the centre of the pitch. Opposition players must be outside the centre circle, on their side of the pitch, when the other team is taking a kick off.

GLOSSARY

ATTACKER – A player whose main objective is to score goals and create scoring chances for others.

BACKPASS – A ball played backwards to a player or to his own goalkeeper.

CHIP – A lofted pass or shot.

CORNER KICK – A ball kicked from the point where the touchline meets the dead-ball line after the ball has gone out of play over the dead-ball line (a defending player having touched it last).

DEFENDER – A player who generally plays close to his own team's goal whose main objective is to prevent the opposition from scoring.

FOUL – Any piece of play or incident on the pitch that contravenes the rules and regulations of the game.

GOAL – A point-scoring play achieved when the ball legally crosses the goal line, under the crossbar and between the posts. The word is also used for the actual structure created by posts, crossbar and a net.

GOALKEEPER – He is responsible for preventing the opposition's ball from entering the net and scoring a goal. The only player on the pitch who is allowed to use his hands to play the ball. He can move anywhere on the pitch but cannot handle the ball outside his team's penalty area.

HEADER – Legal playing of the ball with the head, usually the forehead.

LAY-OFF – Short pass into the path of a team-mate.

MIDFIELDER – A player who generally plays in the space between his team's attack and defence, combining the roles of attacker and defender.

PASS – An intentional ball played to a team-mate.

SAVE – A play made when a goalkeeper successfully intercepts a strike on goal.

SHOT – An attempt at goal.

THROW-IN – A two-armed overhead throw from the touchline, used after the ball has gone out of play.

VOLLEY – A kick where the foot meets the ball in the air before it touches the ground.

WALL – A voluntary line-up of defenders to protect their goal at a free kick. Must be at least 9 metres (10 yds) from the ball.

LISTINGS

FIFA (International football governing body)
FIFA House, PO Box 85, Hitzigweg II,
CH-8030 Zurich, Switzerland
Tel: +41 1 3849595 Fax: +41 1 3849696
Website: www.fifa.com

UEFA (European football governing body)
Jupiterstrasse 33, PO Box 16, 3000 Berne 15, Switzerland
Tel: +41 319 414 121 Fax: +41 319 411 838
Website: www.uefa.com

CONCACAF (North and Central America and Caribbean football governing body)
717 Fifth Avenue, 13th floor, New York, NY 10022, USA

English Football Association
16 Lancaster Gate, London W2 3LW, UK
Tel: +44 20 7262 4542 Fax: +44 20 7402 0486
Website: www.the-fa.org

US Soccer Federation
1801-1811 S. Prarie Ave, Chicago Il 60616, USA
Tel: +1 312 808 1300 Fax: +1 312 808 9535